MENTAL HEALTH GUIDES

UNDERSTANDING
PANIC ATTACKS

by Alexis Burling

BrightPoint Press

San Diego, CA

© 2021 BrightPoint Press
an imprint of ReferencePoint Press, Inc.
Printed in the United States

For more information, contact:
BrightPoint Press
PO Box 27779
San Diego, CA 92198
www.BrightPointPress.com

ALL RIGHTS RESERVED.

No part of this work covered by the copyright hereon may be reproduced or used in any form or by any means—graphic, electronic, or mechanical, including photocopying, recording, taping, web distribution, or information storage retrieval systems—without the written permission of the publisher.

Content Consultant: Michael J. Zvolensky, PhD; Hugh Roy and Lillie Cranz Cullen Distinguished University Professor; Director, Anxiety and Health Research Laboratory/Substance Use Treatment Clinic, University of Houston

---

LIBRARY OF CONGRESS CATALOGING-IN-PUBLICATION DATA

Names: Burling, Alexis, author.
Title: Understanding panic attacks / by Alexis Burling.
Description: San Diego, CA : ReferencePoint Press, [2021] | Series: Mental health guides | Includes bibliographical references and index. | Audience: Grades 10-12
Identifiers: LCCN 2020002430 (print) | LCCN 2020002431 (eBook) | ISBN 9781682829899 (hardcover) | ISBN 9781682829905 (eBook)
Subjects: LCSH: Panic attacks--Juvenile literature.
Classification: LCC RC535 .B867 2021 (print) | LCC RC535 (eBook) | DDC 616.85/223--dc23
LC record available at https://lccn.loc.gov/2020002430
LC eBook record available at https://lccn.loc.gov/2020002431

CONTENTS

AT A GLANCE	4
INTRODUCTION EMMA'S STORY	6
CHAPTER ONE WHAT ARE PANIC ATTACKS?	14
CHAPTER TWO HOW DO PANIC ATTACKS AFFECT PEOPLE?	30
CHAPTER THREE HOW DO PANIC ATTACKS AFFECT SOCIETY?	40
CHAPTER FOUR HOW ARE PANIC ATTACKS TREATED?	56
Glossary	74
Source Notes	75
For Further Research	76
Index	78
Image Credits	79
About the Author	80

AT A GLANCE

- Panic attacks are uncontrollable feelings of intense fear and anxiety.

- There are two types of panic attacks. Uncued panic attacks are unexpected. Cued panic attacks are expected.

- Cued panic attacks are triggered by a frightening situation. They may also be triggered by stress.

- Most panic attacks peak after about ten minutes. They generally last less than thirty minutes.

- Panic attack symptoms may include fast breathing and sweating. A person's heart rate increases.

- Some people suffer from frequent panic attacks. They live in fear of these attacks. This fear affects their daily lives. They have panic disorder (PD).

- Each year, about 6 million US adults struggle with PD. PD usually develops between the ages of eighteen and twenty-five. The average age when people first have symptoms is between twenty and twenty-four years old.

- PD is more common among women. Women are two to three times more likely to develop PD than men.

- Panic attacks can be treated. The best treatments are psychotherapy and medication.

INTRODUCTION

EMMA'S STORY

Emma Stone is a well-known actress. She has starred in hit movies such as *La La Land*. But long before Stone became a celebrity, she suffered from panic attacks. Panic attacks are feelings of intense fear and anxiety. These feelings are uncontrollable. They often come without warning.

Actress Emma Stone has struggled with panic attacks since the age of seven.

Stone's first panic attack happened at age seven. She was at a friend's house. Suddenly, she thought the house was on fire. Her heart raced. Her palms felt sweaty. She could not relax. Stone worried the house would burn down. She thought her life was in danger.

Stone soon realized that the house was not on fire. But she was still spooked. She called her mom and cried. She told her mom about her experience. Stone wanted the scary feelings to go away.

For the next three years, Stone continued to have panic attacks. She often went to the nurse's office at school during lunch. Her fears followed her throughout the day. She says, "I would ask my mom to tell me

Emma Stone works with the Child Mind Institute, which provides resources for children with mental illness.

exactly how the day was going to be. . . . I just needed to know that no one was going to die and nothing was going to change."[1]

Today, Stone still has panic attacks from time to time. But she has learned how to

Panic attacks can come on suddenly and do not always have a clear cause.

handle her anxiety. She goes to therapy and meditates. She talks openly about her struggles. She helps raise awareness of mental health issues. Stone shares her story so that others might feel less alone.

PANIC ATTACKS AND PANIC DISORDER

Many people experience panic attacks. Some have panic **disorder** (PD). They have frequent panic attacks. Each year, about 6 million US adults struggle with PD. That is nearly 3 percent of the US population. About 5 percent of US adults will have PD at some point in their lives.

Panic attacks are frightening. A person's heart beats fast. He may have difficulty breathing. He may think he is having a heart attack. The fear may be so intense that he thinks he might die. But panic attacks are treatable. Seeking professional help is important. Treatment can help reduce people's **symptoms**. Long-term recovery is possible.

Panic attacks are scary and can be painful. But most last only twenty to thirty minutes.

CHAPTER ONE

WHAT ARE PANIC ATTACKS?

Certain life events can cause anxiety. These events are called stressors. They make people feel worried and tense. For example, an exam can be a stressor. People might worry they will do poorly on the test. This feeling is normal.

But some people react more strongly to stressful situations. Barbara O. Rothbaum

Stressors such as tests make most people anxious. However, stressors can cause some people to have panic attacks.

is a professor of psychiatry. Psychiatrists treat people who have mental health issues. Rothbaum explains, "We all physically respond to **stress**. . . . But someone who suffers from panic disorder may react to those same . . . pressures with an exaggerated physical reaction."[2] People who have PD have a strong emotional reaction to stress. They feel intense fear. Their senses are heightened. Rothbaum compares it to the fear someone might experience if he were to come face-to-face with a tiger.

TYPES OF PANIC ATTACKS

Not all people suffer from the same types of panic attacks. Some panic attacks are expected. They are called cued panic attacks. A cue is a sign that something will happen. People may know a certain situation will **trigger** a panic attack.

Panic attacks can be cued or uncued. Prediciting when an uncued panic attack will strike is harder than predicting a cued one.

For example, people who have phobias may have panic attacks. A phobia is a strong fear of something. Some people fear enclosed spaces. They might have a panic attack in an elevator. Aerophobia is also common. It is a fear of flying. People who have aerophobia might have a panic attack on an airplane. Just thinking about a phobia could cause a panic attack.

Some people have uncued panic attacks. These attacks are unexpected. For example, someone might be asleep. Or she might be reading a book. A minor change takes place in her body. Her heart rate may increase. She does not notice this change. But it triggers a panic attack. The attack seems to happen without warning. However, there were signs that an attack might happen. The person just did not detect them.

Other people experience situationally predisposed panic attacks. This means they are more likely to have a panic attack in a frightening situation. But it does not always happen. For example, many people have a

NIGHTTIME PANIC ATTACKS

Some people experience panic attacks at night. These panic attacks wake them up from sleep. The attacks have no obvious trigger or cause. The symptoms are the same as panic attacks that happen during the day. People may sweat and shake. They may be short of breath. Nighttime panic attacks usually last only a few minutes. But it can be hard to go back to sleep afterward.

Someone with a phobia may avoid the places or situations they fear in order to avoid having panic attacks.

fear of social situations. But that does not mean they will have a panic attack every time they go to a party. Some people might have a panic attack only if the party is full of strangers. Or they might have a panic attack hours after the party is over. It can be difficult to know when the next panic attack might strike.

All panic attacks start slowly. First, people start to feel uneasy. Their nervousness builds. The worst symptoms often happen within ten minutes. Then the uncomfortable feelings start to fade. A panic attack is usually over within thirty minutes. An attack rarely lasts longer than an hour.

RELATED DISORDERS

Not all people who have panic attacks have a disorder. Many people have only a few panic attacks in their lifetime. But some people have PD. Panic attacks can occur with other mental disorders too. People with post-traumatic stress disorder (PTSD) may have panic attacks. PTSD is triggered by a terrifying event. Soldiers may develop PTSD after fighting in a war. Certain sounds or sights might remind them of the war. They might have flashbacks. For example, they might hear a loud sound. The sound could remind them of a gun firing. Then they might have a panic attack.

Fear and stress are part of many mental disorders. For example, many people have eating disorders (EDs). They have unhealthy eating behaviors. They may eat too much

Between 11 and 20 percent of veterans from the Iraq and Afghanistan wars are diagnosed with PTSD in a given year. PTSD can trigger panic attacks.

or too little. They feel stressed around food. They might have a panic attack when they are near food. Or they might have a panic attack when they think about weighing themselves.

PD is a type of anxiety disorder. Panic attacks can happen with other anxiety disorders too. A phobia is another type of anxiety disorder. Some people with agoraphobia also have PD. Nearly 2 million US adults have agoraphobia. They fear places where they might not be able to

ASTHMA AND PANIC ATTACKS

A panic attack is a response to stress. These attacks can occur with many types of health conditions. For example, some people have asthma. Asthma is a medical condition. It reduces airflow to the lungs. This makes it hard to breathe. Asthma attacks can be frightening. They can trigger panic attacks.

escape. They may be afraid of crowds. They may also fear enclosed spaces such as buses. This fear triggers a panic attack. People become even more fearful of these situations after a panic attack. Their fear continues to build. After a while, they avoid these places or situations altogether. In extreme cases, people might stop leaving their homes.

Some people with PD use substances such as drugs and alcohol. They mistakenly think it will make their symptoms go away. They develop substance use disorders (SUDs). Substance abuse can make panic attacks happen more often. They can also make the symptoms worse.

PANIC DISORDER

Certain people can **diagnose** mental disorders. They are called mental health professionals. They look at a person's symptoms. Their training helps them identify if someone has a disorder. The *Diagnostic and Statistical Manual of Mental Disorders* (*DSM*) can help them make a diagnosis. The *DSM* lists the symptoms of different disorders. People must have certain symptoms to be diagnosed with PD. The *DSM* lists thirteen possible symptoms.

People must have at least four, such as sweating and chest pain.

People with PD have regular and unexpected panic attacks. They live in fear of these attacks. This period of worry

> ### GISELE BÜNDCHEN'S STORY
>
> Supermodel Gisele Bündchen experienced regular panic attacks. She lived in fear of these attacks. This fear caused a lot of distress. At one point, Bündchen thought about killing herself. But she lived through this experience. She wrote a book about her experiences with PD. The book was published in 2018. Bündchen said, "My intention in writing this book is to . . . help others who may be going through similar experiences."
>
> Quoted in Margaret Jaworski, "Beyond the Beauty: Gisele Bündchen Opens Up About Her Panic Attacks," *Pyscom, April 11, 2019.* www.psycom.net.

usually lasts at least one month. This fear affects people's daily lives. Some people with PD have panic attacks every day. Others go weeks or months between panic attacks.

    Model Gisele Bündchen has PD. She had her first panic attack in 2003. She was twenty-three years old. It happened when she was flying in a small airplane. The flight was bumpy. Bündchen thought the plane would crash. This triggered a panic attack.

    The airplane landed safely. But afterward, Bündchen developed a fear of enclosed spaces. She had panic attacks at work.

At least 19 million adults in the United States suffer from phobias. These can trigger panic attacks.

Being in elevators and on subway trains scared her. She said, "I felt powerless. Your world becomes smaller and smaller, and you can't breathe. . ."[3] She began to have panic attacks at home too. But she later went through treatment. Treatment helped. Over time, her panic attacks went away.

CHAPTER TWO

HOW DO PANIC ATTACKS AFFECT PEOPLE?

A panic attack can strike at any time. It can happen at home or while driving a car. It can occur at work or school.

Fear is a normal response to a threat. The brain activates the fight-flight-freeze response. It sends signals to the rest of the body. The heart beats faster. More blood

Many people have only a few panic attacks during their lives. But people who have them more frequently may worry about when the next attack will occur.

flows to the muscles. Extra oxygen goes to the brain. This makes people alert. Their senses become sharper. Their breathing quickens. All of these changes happen in an instant. They prepare the body to react to a threat. People may stay and fight the threat. Or they may run away. But in some cases, people find it hard to move. They freeze, or stay in the same spot.

The brain activates the fight-flight-freeze response during a panic attack. Panic attacks usually happen when there is no threat. People are not in danger. But they react as if they are.

The nervous system is involved in the fight-flight-freeze response. The nerves and the brain make up the nervous system. Normally part of the nervous system kicks in after a person feels fear. It lowers her

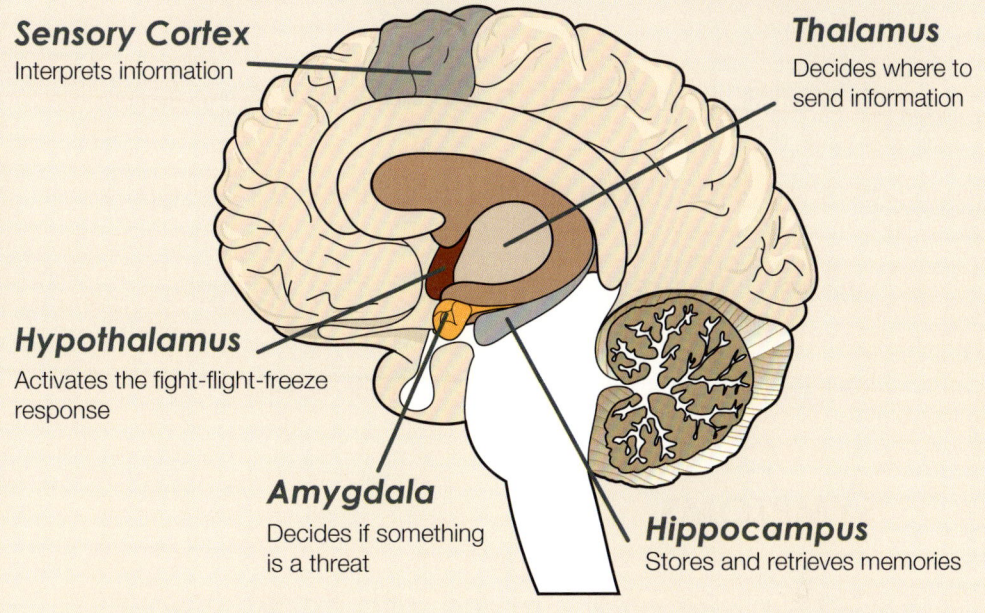

This illustration shows how the brain responds to something fearful. Many parts of the brain are involved in the fear response.

heart rate and blood pressure. This helps her calm down. But when a panic attack happens, something goes wrong. Paul Li is a professor of cognitive science. Cognitive science is the study of the mind and how it works. Li says, "If the . . . nervous system is somehow unable to do its job, a person will remain fired up."[4] It takes the person longer to recover from the fear response.

SYMPTOMS

Certain symptoms come with panic attacks. Most are mild. They go away quickly. Others can seem life-threatening even though they are not. Some symptoms are physical. People feel as if the world around them is spinning. Their throat tightens. It becomes harder to breathe. They may feel like they are having a heart attack.

People may also sweat during a panic attack. Their hands or limbs may shake. Kendra Cherry is a mental health specialist. She explains, "Your muscles become tense and primed for action. This tension can result in trembling or shaking."[5]

PANIC ATTACKS VERSUS HEART ATTACKS

People may mistake a panic attack for a heart attack. It can be hard for them to tell the difference. But the symptoms are slightly different. The pain in a panic attack is sharp. People feel this pain in the middle of their chest. People also have pain during a heart attack. But it feels more like heavy pressure. It extends from the jaw down to the arm. Heart attack symptoms usually last longer. They also get worse over time.

Panic attacks have similar symptoms to many medical conditions. Someone who has had a panic attack should talk to a doctor to rule out other conditions.

People who have frequent panic attacks often have chest pain. They might feel nauseated. Shallow breathing causes dizziness. People may feel a numbness in their feet. Some people's body temperature changes. They get suddenly cold. Or they may feel too warm. Panic attacks can also cause headaches.

Other panic attack symptoms are psychological. Panic attacks affect people's thoughts. People fear they will lose control. They may feel like they are floating above their own body. They may think they are going to die. But people cannot die from panic attacks.

CAUSES

Panic attacks happen when people perceive a threat. Some experts think stress also plays a role. People with PD might have experienced something troubling in their childhood. For example, a family member might have died. A reminder of the event can trigger a panic attack.

In other cases, something stressful happens to someone in the present. The person does not know how to cope. For example, a student might have a conflict at school. Stress builds quickly. Then he has a panic attack.

Research also shows that panic attacks and PD can run in families. People who have relatives with PD may be more likely to develop PD. Personality could be a factor too. Some people are more sensitive to stressors than others. They experience more negative emotions. These people are more prone to panic attacks.

JAKE'S STORY

Jake had his first panic attack when he was in high school. He was an excellent student. But the pressure to succeed started to get to him. One day, his parents found him curled up on his bedroom floor. He thought about suicide. It took a year of therapy for him to get better. Medication also helped. Jake learned how to cope with his fear. He says, "The future has reopened its doors."

Quoted in Benoit Denizet-Lewis, "Why Are More American Teenagers Than Ever Suffering from Severe Anxiety?" New York Times, October 11, 2017. www.nytimes.com.

CHAPTER THREE

HOW DO PANIC ATTACKS AFFECT SOCIETY?

About one in seventy-five Americans will be diagnosed with PD. PD usually develops in young adults. Many people develop symptoms between the ages of eighteen and twenty-five. But PD can occur in people of any age. Older adults can be diagnosed with PD.

Genes play a part in who develops PD. Someone who has an immediate family member with PD is more likely to develop it as well.

Teenagers can have PD. Children can experience PD-like symptoms. Their symptoms are usually less intense. Kids are rarely diagnosed with PD.

Panic attacks happen to people of all races. But ethnic groups may experience

Men and women can have different panic attack symptoms. Men are more likely to report pain, while women report issues with breathing.

panic attacks differently. Some studies have found this to be the case. For example, Latinx people may pay greater attention to physical symptoms. Black and white Americans' experiences may differ too. African Americans are more likely to report numbness and tingling. Experts are not sure why this is.

Gender can also influence how people experience panic attacks. Women often have more frequent panic attacks. Their symptoms are usually worse. Women and men may also have different symptoms. Men are more likely to sweat. They are

> **GENDER DIFFERENCES**
>
> PD is more common among women than among men. Women are two to three times more likely to have PD. It is also more common among women who have never been pregnant. Women who have been pregnant and develop PD usually do so after giving birth, not during pregnancy.

more likely to have stomach or chest pain.

Women usually experience more shaking.

They may have more difficulty breathing.

DEALING WITH STIGMA

People who have panic attacks face many challenges. They may have to deal with stigma. Stigma is a mark of shame or embarrassment. People with mental illness often face stigma. This is because many people misunderstand them. But a 2018 **survey** shows that this attitude may be changing. Researchers surveyed US adults. The adults were between the ages of thirty-five and sixty-four. Eighty-seven percent said having a mental illness is nothing to be ashamed of. Eighty-six percent believed people with mental illnesses can get better. However, some stigma still exists. In the 2018 survey, people answered statements. One statement was, "People with mental health disorders scare me." One-third of the respondents agreed

People who struggle with PD may have to deal with stigma. This can lower a person's self-esteem.

with this statement. Thirty-nine percent said they would view someone differently if they knew that person had a mental illness. Only 35 percent said they would let a mentally ill person care for their child.

Luna Greenstein writes about mental health issues. She explains how stigma affects people who have mental illnesses. She says, "Stigma causes people to feel ashamed for something that *is* out of their control. Worst of all, stigma prevents people from seeking the help they need. . . . [S]tigma is an unacceptable addition to their pain."[6]

AT SCHOOL AND IN THE WORKPLACE

Panic attacks can affect many parts of a person's life. Students can have panic attacks. Panic attacks can affect their self-confidence. The students may feel

A job often creates stress. It is important for someone who suffers from panic attacks to find coping mechanisms they can do in the workplace.

ashamed. They might also live in fear of the next attack. They might find it hard to concentrate. Fear affects their ability to learn. It can also affect their ability to plan and manage their time. Their grades may drop as a result. They might get passed over for leadership positions in sports or clubs.

Panic attacks can affect people in the workplace too. They could affect someone's chances of getting hired for a job. Most people feel nervous before a job interview. The fear of a panic attack can make people feel even more nervous. Their symptoms may flare up. The anxiety could negatively affect their performance in the interview.

Panic attacks could also interfere with job promotions. People who take on more projects are more likely to get promoted.

But a large workload can create stress. This stress could cause a panic attack. People with PD might not volunteer to work on new projects. They do not want to trigger a panic attack.

Katharina Star is a counselor. She treats people who have anxiety disorders. She

> **EMPLOYEE ASSISTANCE PROGRAMS**
>
> Many companies offer employee assistance programs. These programs can help employees who are struggling with certain issues. The issues include stress and mental illness. The programs are free. Most take place at work. People first answer a series of questions. This helps identify the illness or issue. The results are not shared with anyone. Counseling sessions are also part of the programs.

says, "You may feel worried . . . that your panic secret will be revealed. You may be very concerned about having a panic attack in front of your coworkers or, worse, your boss."[7] The threat of panic attacks can add a lot of stress to a person's workday.

PANIC ATTACKS AND RELATIONSHIPS

Panic attacks can affect people's relationships as well. People often avoid situations that might trigger an attack. They might avoid social gatherings. They might quit a school sport or club. They become isolated. They withdraw from relationships. They spend less time with family and friends. They may feel lonely. They might have suicidal thoughts.

People may not know how to help a loved one who has panic attacks. They might not understand the symptoms. Or they might think the person is overreacting. They might tell the person to relax. But many therapists say this is the worst thing to do. Meghan Reid has panic attacks. She has been in this situation. She says,

[M]y family kept telling me to just 'relax.' Telling someone who is in a panic attack to just relax is basically useless. The best advice I can give

If someone nearby has a panic attack, it is important to stay calm and offer support. One way to help is to count to ten with the person to encourage slower breathing.

is to just listen to the person having the panic attack on what his or her needs are.[8]

People with PD will sometimes isolate themselves from others to avoid having panic attacks.

Panic attacks affect people in different ways. The symptoms can differ from person to person. It can be hard for people who have never had a panic attack to understand what it feels like. Most mental health experts say the best way to help is to be patient. Loved ones should learn how to listen and be supportive. Dina Cagliostro is a psychologist. She treats people who have mental illnesses. She explains how people can be supportive when someone has a panic attack. She says, "Assure them that this attack is only temporary and they will get through it."[9] Loved ones can also encourage people to seek help. Treatment can help people manage the disorder.

CHAPTER FOUR

HOW ARE PANIC ATTACKS TREATED?

People who have had a panic attack should visit a doctor. Doctors can help figure out what the problem is. It may be PD. But other conditions have similar symptoms. This often makes PD difficult to diagnose. Doctors may mistake PD for another health condition. People may also

Mental health professionals can diagnose PD. They can also help arrange for treatment after a diagnosis.

not realize they are experiencing a panic attack. They may think they have a heart condition. Then people may not get the treatment they need. So it is important for patients and doctors to know the signs of PD.

The first step is to get a physical exam. A doctor gives this exam. An exam may help rule out other health issues. Then the doctor

OTHER CONDITIONS

Panic attacks can be difficult to diagnose. Other conditions may have similar symptoms. Some people have a heart condition. One of the heart's valves does not close correctly. This condition causes chest pain. Another issue is hyperthyroidism. This condition happens when the thyroid gland is overactive. This causes sweating and shakiness. Low blood sugar is another problem. People who have low blood sugar become lightheaded. Panic attacks are also sometimes confused with asthma.

does a blood test. She checks for signs of heart disease. She also asks about a person's symptoms and family history. The doctor may not find any signs of a health condition. She may recommend a mental health professional. This professional can make a diagnosis.

There are many ways to treat panic attacks and PD. Treatment lessens the symptoms of a panic attack. It can also help prevent future attacks. The goal of treatment is to improve people's quality of life. The main treatment for panic attacks is psychotherapy.

Psychotherapy is one of the most effective forms of treatment for panic attacks. Patients learn to lower stress and manage their anxiety.

PSYCHOTHERAPY

Some mental health professionals can provide psychotherapy. They are called therapists. Many types of professionals can be therapists. For example, counselors and psychologists can be therapists. Psychotherapy is a process. It involves many sessions. Therapists talk to people about their thoughts and actions. They help people change their negative thought patterns. They also help people become less afraid of their symptoms. For example, therapists may help people realize they will not die from a panic attack. In addition, therapists help people find ways to manage their stress. Then people might have fewer panic attacks.

One type of psychotherapy is cognitive behavioral therapy (CBT). CBT often helps people who have panic attacks. CBT sessions usually happen one-on-one. Patients talk about what triggers their panic attacks. Therapists put them in a situation that could trigger an attack. Or they ask the patient to imagine something that could trigger an attack. But they do this in a safe environment. They often do this exercise in the therapist's office. This part of CBT is called exposure therapy. People talk through their experience. They explore what makes their panic attacks scary. They learn ways to cope with the attacks. Their fear of future attacks may fade over time.

Jerry Bubrick is a psychologist. He uses CBT to treat people who have anxiety disorders. He asks his patients to do jumping jacks. Or he asks them to spin around until they are dizzy. They repeat this process over and over. Then they do deep-breathing exercises. These exercises send more oxygen to the brain.

TREATMENT COSTS

CBT sessions usually last forty-five minutes to an hour. The cost can range from $100 to more than $250 per session. Prescription drugs are expensive too. A supply can cost more than $200 without insurance. Some therapists offer sliding scale payment options. The cost is based on the patient's **income**. People who do not make much money will pay less.

Deep breathing is one coping skill. It can calm a person's mind. It can slow a person's heart rate. Over time, the feeling of panic seems less threatening. People gradually move on to scarier situations. For example, people who have agoraphobia might try riding a bus. They have developed coping skills. These skills help them manage their fear. People may become more confident in these situations.

The length of treatment varies. Some people see progress after ten weekly sessions. Others may need to stay in therapy longer. Panic attacks might still

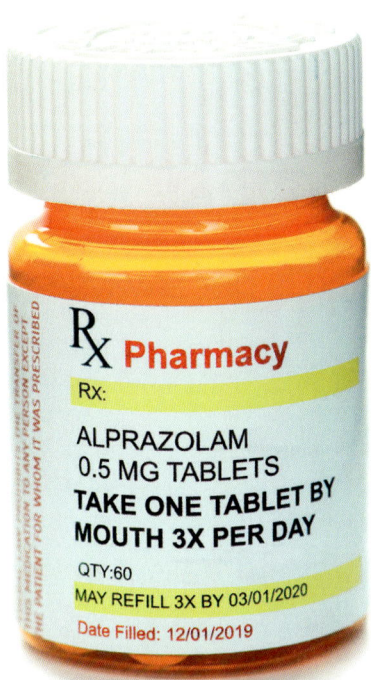

Some people find medication helpful to manage their symptoms. However, some anti-anxiety medications are only intened for short-term use.

reoccur for months or a few years. In these situations, people may also take medication.

MEDICATION

CBT is the most effective treatment for PD. But CBT alone may not work for some people. They may need medication too. Medication is not always necessary for panic attacks. Most doctors advise against taking anything if just one attack occurred. But medication can help some people who have PD. It can reduce their symptoms. Doctors can **prescribe** medication. So can psychiatrists. Psychiatrists are mental health professionals.

Antidepressants can help some people with PD. They can lower people's anxiety levels. Doctors tell people how to take the medication. People may have to try different types of medication before they find the right one. Medication works best when paired with therapy. It should never be taken without a prescription.

Andrea Petersen has PD. She is a reporter for the *Wall Street Journal*. She says antidepressants helped her. She explains, "I find myself more present in the

ANTI-ANXIETY PILLS

Antidepressants may not help some people who have PD. They may be prescribed anti-anxiety pills. These pills calm part of the person's nervous system. People take these pills only on a short-term basis. The pills can have bad side effects if taken with other medication. People can also become addicted to these pills. Doctors usually do not prescribe these pills to people who have had SUDs.

Relaxation techniques such as yoga or meditation can help relieve stress. This helps prevent panic attacks.

moment, able to have conversations."[10] She spends less time worrying. She is able to focus more on her relationships.

Benzodiazepines are another type of medication. They may also help people with PD. They can reduce anxiety. But people usually take them just in the short term. Long-term use can have side effects. People may become dependent on them. So doctors do not prescribe them for people who have had SUDs.

LIFESTYLE CHANGES AND GROUP THERAPY

Lifestyle changes may also help people who have panic attacks. Substance abuse can contribute to panic attacks. Drugs and alcohol can make it more difficult for people

There are many types of group therapy. Some groups are only for PD, while others are more general, such as a group for anxiety disorders.

to handle stressful situations. Doctors recommend avoiding alcohol and drugs. Getting plenty of sleep is also important. People are more likely to become anxious when they do not get enough sleep.

Regular exercise can help relieve stress. Yoga and meditation can also help in some cases. When people meditate, they focus on their body. They close their eyes. They try to relax. They become more aware of their thoughts. They let negative thoughts pass. This practice can help reduce anxiety.

Some people go to group therapy. Group therapy involves talking to others who have similar issues. Support groups may also be helpful. These groups are made of people with similar experiences. People can find a supportive community. This can help them feel less alone.

PD can never be completely cured. But with treatment and support, it becomes easier to manage.

People with PD can get better with the right treatment. About 40 percent of people with PD become symptom-free for long periods. Another 50 percent experience only mild symptoms. These symptoms do not affect their daily life. Mark Markham has panic attacks. Group therapy helped him deal with these attacks. The therapy program lasted three weeks. He learned how to meditate. He also practiced breathing exercises. He says, "[T]here isn't a magic pill. But with the right [treatment], I have found that you can live a fulfilled life."[11]

GLOSSARY

diagnose

to identify an illness or condition based on its symptoms

disorder

a physical or mental condition that affects a person's ability to function and causes distress

prescribe

to write a prescription, or an official recommendation that tells someone which medicine to take

stress

a feeling of pressure or tension

survey

a questionnaire that helps researchers understand people's ideas and beliefs

symptoms

the signs of an illness or disorder

trigger

to cause or set in motion

SOURCE NOTES

INTRODUCTION

1. Quoted in Leigh Weingus, "7 Celebrities Describe What It's Like to Suffer a Panic Attack," *HuffPost*, June 24, 2015. www.huffpost.com.

CHAPTER ONE: WHAT ARE PANIC ATTACKS?

2. Quoted in "Under Pressure," *MedicineNet*, January 31, 2006. www.medicinenet.com.

3. Quoted in Erica Gonzales, "Gisele Bündchen Reveals She Had Severe Panic Attacks During Her Modeling Career," *Harper's Bazaar*, September 27, 2018. www.harpersbazaar.com.

CHAPTER TWO: HOW DO PANIC ATTACKS AFFECT PEOPLE?

4. Paul Li, "What Happens in the Brain When We Experience a Panic Attack?" *Scientific American*, July 1, 2011. www.scientificamerican.com.

5. Kendra Cherry, "How the Fight or Flight Response Works," *Verywell Mind*, August 18, 2019. www.verywellmind.com.

CHAPTER THREE: HOW DO PANIC ATTACKS AFFECT SOCIETY?

6. Luna Greenstein, "9 Ways to Fight Mental Health Stigma," *NAMI*, October 11, 2017. www.nami.org.

7. Katharina Star, "Managing Your Panic Disorder at Work," *Verywell Mind*, April 10, 2020. www.verywellmind.com.

8. Quoted in Lindsay Holmes, "What You Should Know if You Love Someone Who Has Panic Attacks," *HuffPost*, March 16, 2018. www.huffpost.com.

9. Dina Cagliostro, "Panic Attacks & Panic Disorder: Symptoms, Causes, and Treatment," *Psycom*, February 24, 2020. www.psycom.net.

CHAPTER FOUR: HOW ARE PANIC ATTACKS TREATED?

10. Quoted in Caroline Miller, "Panic Attacks and How to Treat Them," *Child Mind Institute*, n.d. www.childmind.org.

11. Mark Markham, "Breaking the Silence and Stigma of Mental Illness," *Mayo Clinic*, October 18, 2019. www.sharing.mayoclinic.org.

FOR FURTHER RESEARCH

BOOKS

Holly Duhig, *A Book About Anxiety*. New York: PowerKids Press, 2020.

Jennifer Lombardo, *Anxiety and Panic Disorders*. New York: Lucent Press, 2018.

Celina McManus, *Understanding Anxiety*. San Diego, CA: ReferencePoint Press, 2021.

Hilary W. Poole, *Anxiety Disorders*. New York: AV2 by Weigl, 2019.

INTERNET SOURCES

"Panic Attacks and Panic Disorder," *Mayo Clinic*, May 4, 2018. www.mayoclinic.org.

"Panic Disorder: When Fear Overwhelms," *National Institute of Mental Health*, 2016. www.nimh.nih.gov.

Katharina Star, "An Overview of Panic Attack Types and Symptoms," *Verywell Mind*, October 20, 2019. www.verywellmind.com.

WEBSITES

Child Mind Institute
www.childmind.org

This site shares resources to help children who have mental health and learning disorders.

KidsHealth
www.kidshealth.org

This site contains resources for kids, teens, and parents. KidsHealth shares information about anxiety disorders and other mental health issues.

National Institute of Mental Health (NIMH)
www.nimh.nih.gov

The NIMH site offers information about different types of mental illnesses, including panic disorder.

INDEX

anxiety, 4, 6, 11, 14, 23–24, 49–50, 63, 66, 69–71
asthma, 24, 58

Bündchen, Gisele, 27, 28–29
Bubrick, Jerry, 63

Cagliostro, Dina, 55
Cherry, Kendra, 35
cognitive behavioral therapy (CBT), 61–63, 65
coping skills, 39, 62, 64
costs, 63
counselors, 50, 60
cued panic attacks, 4, 16–18

Diagnostic and Statistical Manual of Mental Disorders (DSM), 26

eating disorders (EDs), 22–23
employee assistance programs, 50
ethnicity, 41–43

fight-flight-freeze response, 30–32

gender, 43–44
Greenstein, Luna, 47
group therapy, 71, 73

heart attacks, 12, 34, 35

Li, Paul, 33–34

Markham, Mark, 73
medication, 5, 39, 65–69

Petersen, Andrea, 67–68
phobias, 17–18, 24, 64
post-traumatic stress disorder (PTSD), 22
psychiatrists, 15, 66
psychologists, 55, 61, 63
psychotherapy, 5, 59, 60–65

Reid, Meghan, 52–53
Rothbaum, Barbara O., 14–16

Star, Katharina, 50–51
stigma, 44–47
Stone, Emma, 4–11
stress, 4, 14–16, 22–23, 24, 37–39, 50–51, 61, 70–71
substance use disorders (SUDs), 25, 67, 69
symptoms, 4–5, 12, 18, 19, 21, 25–26, 34–37, 40–43, 49, 52, 54, 56, 58, 59, 61, 66, 73

therapists, 52, 60–62, 63
triggers, 4, 16, 18, 19, 22, 24, 25, 28, 38, 50–51, 62,

uncued panic attacks, 4, 18

IMAGE CREDITS

Cover: © fizkes/Shutterstock Images
5: © panitanphoto/Shutterstock Images
7: © Featureflash Photo Agency/Shutterstock Images
9: © Tinseltown/Shutterstock Images
10: © Stuart Jenner/Shutterstock Images
13: © pixelfit/iStockphoto
15: © antoniodiaz/Shutterstock Images
17: © Tero Vesalainen/Shutterstock Images
20: © tommaso79/Shutterstock Images
23: © Photographee.eu/Shutterstock Images
29: © Atstock Productions/Shutterstock Images
31: © Adam Gregor/Shutterstock Images
33: © Blamb/Shutterstock Images
36: © Iakov Filimonov/Shutterstock Images
41: © ruigsantos/Shutterstock Images
42: © Ranta Images/Shutterstock Images
46: © Sweet Memento Photography/Shutterstock Images
48: © Aleksandra Suzi/Shuttestock Images
53: © Motortion Films/Shutterstock Images
54: © panitanphoto/Shutterstock Images
57: © Photographee.eu/Shutterstock Images
60: © wavebreakmedia/Shutterstock Images
65: © Sherry Yates Young/Shutterstock Images
68: © dualstock/iStockphoto
70: © AnnaStills/iStockphoto
72: © Nikola Ilic/iStockphoto

ABOUT THE AUTHOR

Alexis Burling has written dozens of articles and books for young readers on a variety of topics ranging from current events and famous people to nutrition and fitness. She is also a book critic. Her book reviews, author interviews, and other industry-related articles have been published in the *New York Times*, the *Washington Post*, and many other sources. Burling lives in Portland, Oregon, with her husband.